Excuse Me, Did You Know Him?

Eight Sermons And
Orders Of Service
For Lent

By Jack Brownlee

CSS Publishing Company, Inc.
Lima, Ohio

EXCUSE ME, DID YOU KNOW HIM?

Copyright © 1994 by
The CSS Publishing Company, Inc.
Lima, Ohio

All rights reserved. If you are the original purchaser, you may copy the orders of service only, no other part of this publication may be reproduced, stored in a retrieval system, or transmitted in any form or by any means, electronic, mechanical, photocopying, recording, or otherwise, without the prior permission of the publisher. Inquiries should be addressed to: The CSS Publishing Company, Inc., 628 South Main Street, Lima, Ohio 45804.

Scripture quotations are from the *Revised Standard Version of the Bible,* copyrighted 1946, 1952, (c), 1971, 1973, by the Division of Christian Education of the National Council of the Churches of Christ in the USA. Used by permission.

Library of Congress Cataloging-in-Publication Data

Brownlee, Jack, 1950-
 Excuse me, did you know him? : eight sermons for the season of Lent / by Jack Brownlee.
  p.   cm.
 1. Lenten sermons. 2. Sermons, American. 3. Lent. 4. Worship programs. I. Title.
BV4277.V765   1994
252'.62—dc20   93-30821
                                                                         CIP

ISBN 978-1-55673-705-3   PRINTED IN U.S.A.

*"For all the Saints,
who from their labors rest ..."*

*For John, for Mary
and mostly for Kenneth*

Table Of Contents

Introduction   7

Lent 1
   Order Of Service   9
   Miriam, Why Not?   11

Lent 2
   Order Of Service   17
   Levi's Song   19

Lent 3
   Order of Service   25
   Zacchaeus   27

Lent 4
   Order Of Service   33
   The Ring   35

Lent 5
   Order Of Service   41
   A Penny's Worth Of Thanks   43

Palm Sunday (Or Maundy Thursday)
   Order Of Service   47
   The Water Boy   49

Good Friday
   Order Of Service   57
   Excuse Me, Did You Know Him?   59

Easter Sunday
   Order of Service   65
   Making Disciples   67

Introduction

From the cosmopolitan city of Sepphoris, to the provincial towns, to the capital city of Jerusalem, Jesus of Nazareth taught and healed as an itinerant Rabbi. His life touched the lives of countless numbers. From the biblical record we have enough evidence to be convinced that he was the Son of the Living God: The Messiah. Others were not convinced. Dozens of nameless people "bumped" into Jesus and his early followers and were left unaffected by his ministry.

These stories are about people like us, who struggle with their jobs, their relationships, their dreams and who did not quite understand the significance of this traveling preacher. They understood something was different, but they were not sure what.

Jewish faith was being transformed during the time of Jesus' ministry, the reliance on the temple and the priesthood was giving way to the Rabbi and the local congregation. The Roman and Greek influences in culture and commerce were creating dis-unity in a religion seeking to be faithful to One God. Agriculture was not the only occupation, and a faith that required grain offerings and allowed gleaning as a way of sharing with the poor struggled to find new ways of expressing faithfulness to God. Far from revitalizing a dying faith, Jesus taught in the midst of this upheaval.

In telling these stories, the presenter may wish to either read them dramatically or retell them in a style fitting the situation. It would also be possible to cut the stories into a group reading script matching voices with individuals in the stories.

Many of the people in these stories are those whom I have met in the performance of ministry over the last 20 years. Clergy in these tales, who are not always seen in the best of light, are colleagues of mine.

Portions of the liturgies used in the worship materials are from *Thankful Praise*, Keith Watkins, Ed. Christian Board of Publication, St. Louis 1987. (reprinted by permission) Appreciation is also expressed to the congregations where these stories found ears.

I especially want to thank my wife, Dorothy (even when she liked the other ending) for hearing these so often. And finally Rev. Tom Felts with whom I have conspired to make faith meaningful.

Jack Brownlee
Moundsville, West Virginia
April 1993

Order Of Service
Lent 1

Opening Words:
L: Let us worship our Creator, the God of Love.
P: God continually preserves and sustains us.
L: We have been forgiven with complete understanding.
P: Through Jesus Christ we have received the full love of God.

Hymn: "How Firm A Foundation"

Prayer Of Confession: *(Unison)*
Forgive my sin and cover my transgression, O Lord. I acknowledge my sin and pray unto thee in a time when thou may be found. Thou art my hiding place, O God. I seek preservation in thy word. Encompass me with the songs of deliverance. Teach me the way my steps should go. Open me to hear your teaching. Keep me from closing my ears to you. Guide me in thy paths. Amen.

Assurance Of Pardon:
Those who trust in the Lord shall have the Lord's mercy encompass them. Be glad in the Lord, and rejoice ye righteous; shout for joy all of you with upright hearts. The Lord will cover your sin and remember it no more. Live forgiven lives.

Readings: Psalm 103:1-13; Luke 4:16-30

Hymn: "Spirit Of God, Descend ..." stanzas 1, 2

Meditation: "Miriam, Why Not?"

Hymn: "Spirit Of God, Descend ..." stanzas 3, 4

Call To Communion:
> L: Let us affirm our faith.
>
> **P: We believe that when the spirit fills us we must respond to the crying needs of the world. We believe that there are many people crying. Some shout in the square at noon. Others whisper alone at night by themselves. The good news is that God hears and sends us, in the name of Christ, to listen and to respond.**
>
> L: Lift up your hearts.
>
> **P: We lift them up to the Lord.**
>
> L: Let us give thanks to the Lord our God.
>
> **P: It is right and good that we give thanks.**

Prayers For Bread And Cup

The Distribution

Dismissal:
> L: It is difficult to admit that we have grown comfortable with our prejudices, but the Lord finds ways to remind us of the unmerited love God has for all.
>
> **P: Let us rejoice in that love knowing that we are part of something greater than ourselves.**
>
> L: Let us go in peace, celebrating the fact that God not only forgives us, but gives us the Spirit to proclaim the good news to all.
>
> **P: May the spirit of God lead us in joy.**

Miriam, Why Not?
Lent 1

"Miriam!"
"Shush."
"Miriam, why not?"
"Huh?"
"Why couldn't he do anything?"
"I don't know."
"Miriam, why couldn't he do anything here?"
"Joshua, I don't know. Go to sleep!"

But he couldn't sleep. Not tonight. He lay upon his mat on the top of the house as he and Miriam usually did in the warm summer, but he could not go to sleep. It was not the sweet smelling light breeze winding its way through the mountain passes on Mount Carmel bringing with them the full and rich smell of the blossoming trees and wild flowers that kept him awake. Nor was it the glorious sight of what seemed to be a million stars dotting God's blue blanket of heaven with the moon illuminating the small puffs of clouds arranged in shapes creating a backdrop for fantastic stories that kept his eyes open. And neither was it the gentle music that floated through the air from the tavern in Nazareth, bothersome in the sense that it would prevent tired eyes from closing from a busy and exciting day. Joshua could not sleep because of what had happened between the men of the village and his friend Jesus that afternoon. It seemed so incredible to a boy of eight that the men, including Father, would be so upset with Jesus. Perhaps Miriam, being 11 and much wiser in the ways of grownups, could answer his questions.

"Miriam, I can't go to sleep."
"Joshua, you better try harder."
"I can't. I keep thinking about him."

"I know."

"Were the stories that we heard about him true?"

"Joshua, I don't know. I thought they were, but ..."

"I mean those people that he healed, and helped. Were the men here upset because he did something or because he didn't ..."

"Joshua, I know he was your friend ..."

"Before he moved to Capernaum, I used to go over to his shop and watch him work with the wood. He could make anything. When we went there he used to give us sweet gums and talk to me and the other boys. He would make us laugh, and feel good and tell us the stories of the kings and prophets and the fathers. When he told them, the stories came alive, and he taught us so much more about the Law than the Rabbi in school did. You felt like ..."

"Joshua, you have to go to sleep."

"And those two chairs he made for us. They look just like the ones his father made for us, but you know yourself that they feel different when you sit in them. You feel like you're loved when you sit in them."

"Joshua, Papa is going to come up here in a minute, and be angry with both of us for talking. We have a lot to do tomorrow, including going to school. Go to sleep!"

"I was scared when they backed him on to the side of the cliff. I didn't know what was going to happen. But he walked right through them, as angry as they were. But he wasn't mad. He was sad. Sad maybe that someplace that had been home was now a place he could not be. Why were they so mad at him?"

"I don't know. We weren't in the synagogue. We don't know what they said. Or what he said."

"But ..."

"All I know is that I overheard someone say that the Rabbi said that Jesus said he was the Messiah. And I guess that's why they were upset. The Messiah wouldn't be a carpenter from Nazareth, would he?"

"I guess not."

"Okay. Go to sleep."
"But you know what, Miriam?"
"What?"
"When he came into town, I felt like he was coming to see me. I felt good inside. And you know what?"
"What?"
"He remembered my name."
"Go to sleep."
"Why couldn't he heal anyone?"
"I don't know. But if you don't go to sleep, you'll have a chance to ask Papa in about five minutes. And I don't think he'll want to talk about it."
"Well, okay. But ..."
"Shush."

"Caleb."
"Huh?"
"Caleb."
"What?"
"The children are awake on the roof. Talking."
"Oh. Okay, I'll ... ah ... go ... talk ..."
"No, Caleb. They are talking about what happened today. With Jesus. Joshua wants to know why."
"Why what?"
"Why the village was so upset with Jesus."
"The guy's an idiot, Mary. A blasphemer."
"What did he do ...?"
"Look, a guy leaves town, leaving his kid brothers to marry off three sisters and take care of his widowed mother. If he makes a name for himself, makes some money, sends some home, helps out, fine. I say fine and dandy."
"Caleb!"
"I'm serious, Mary. If he were teaching but still making a good living in Capernaum, I'd be the first one to say, 'Hey, Jesus, good to see you, welcome back, want to say a few

words?' But for Pete's sake Mary, with the talent he has working with wood, he's wasting himself. Walking around the countryside with fishermen, Zealots, tax collectors, and who knows what else."

"What did he say in the synagogue?"

"Oh! Well he read from the prophet Isaiah, and then made it sound like he was the fulfillment of the prophet's words. Can you believe it, a carpenter from Nazareth the Messiah? For Pete's sake. I'll tell you, Mary, if the guy's gonna be the Messiah, he's gonna have to knock off a few legionnaires and crazy Herod instead of telling people to be friends and walk another mile with a legionnaire's knapsacks. For Pete's sake."

"Okay, maybe he's not the Messiah, but he has become a teacher, and all Rabbis are due respect. He has enabled people to see and walk."

"Mary."

"Why back him up against a cliff?"

"It was blasphemy, that's why. You and the children need protection from that kind of thinking. Not only is it wrong, it is dangerous. If we do nothing, the legion thinks we harbor Zealots. Not because he is one but just because he hangs around with them."

"If you thought that you would have cast him down and stoned him."

"We ..."

"Caleb, there was something more. You know that Jesus has always been more in touch with God than you or I could ever be. Am I right? We've never been quite able to understand him. You know that. And that's not since he moved to Capernaum. He's always been that way."

"I know." Caleb paused to think about his long relationship with Jesus. "One year, when we were young, we all went to Jerusalem for the Passover. Well, he got lost. And no one noticed until we were about a day back. Well, his mother and father went back looking for him. Found him later in the temple, asking questions. Really shocked a few of the priests. Some of them are in the Sanhedrin now. Anyway, Joseph's big strong hands reach out for him, and Joseph says, 'Son, where have you been, we've been worried sick about you?' And Jesus just looked at him. 'Why didn't you know that I was in the temple?' Something like that. He was right, they should have known that was where he'd be. For Pete's sake, that's the way he was.''

"I was expecting him to still be 12. I was expecting him to be Mary and Joseph's son. I was expecting him to be, gosh, I don't know. Why didn't he let us know?"

Mary relaxed, "How would he let you know?"

"I'm not sure!"

"Maybe he didn't let us know because we would have asked for proof, somehow. Heal somebody? Or maybe kill a legionnaire."

"What do I tell Joshua?"

"Tell him that we must have faith that God will redeem us, and that while we don't know if Jesus is the Messiah, we know that there are several ways of being blind."

"And more than one way to be imprisoned. We were wrong to expect Jesus to be other than what he's always been — a friend."

Coming up the steps to the roof, the view of a million stars mingled with the soft breeze and the light music coming from the tavern below. Quietly a shadow moved toward the sleeping mats.

"Joshua ..."

Order Of Service
Lent 2

Opening Words:

    L: Let us worship our Creator, the God of Love.

    P: God continually preserves and sustains us.

    L: We have been forgiven to embrace new life.

    P: Through Jesus Christ we have received the full love of God.

Hymn: "How Firm A Foundation"

Prayer Of Confession:

    Unto thee, O Lord do I lift up my soul. I put my trust in thee, O God. Show thy paths, teach thy ways, lead in thy truth; remember, O Lord, thy tender mercies. Do not remember my sin. Take from me my self justification. Center me in thy will. Open me to thy spirit. Amen.

Assurance Of Pardon:

    The path of the Lord is mercy and truth to those who keep the covenant. Pardon shall be granted from thy iniquity. Deliverance shall keep thy soul, shame shall be kept from thy house. You have placed trust in the Lord. You have waited for the Lord with integrity. You are forgiven.

Readings: Psalm 25:1-7; John 6:1-13

Hymn: "I Need Thee Every Hour" stanzas 1, 2

Meditation: Levi's Song

Hymn: "O Love That Will Not Let Me Go" stanzas 3, 4

Call To Communion:
>L: Let us affirm our faith.
>
>**P: We believe that the eyes of faith see miracles where doubt sees only broken crumbs. The song of faith rises triumphantly over the feelings of being lost in a familiar world. We believe that to end physical and spiritual hunger in the world we must completely offer to God what we have and who we are.**

Prayers For Bread And Cup

The Distribution

Dismissal:
>L: It is difficult to be obedient to God and self-centered at the same time. May we fully enter the new life granted to us by Christ.
>
>**P: Let us rejoice in God, our creator.**
>
>L: May the Spirit of God lead us in joy.
>
>**P: Amen.**

Levi's Song
Lent 2

Levi hummed his favorite song as he walked toward home from the marketplace. The tune to the psalm matched his mood on this wonderful sunny day. The breeze was warm, but not too warm. The sun was bright, but not so that you needed to squint. The air was scented with the aromas of the marketplace, each step bringing a whiff of date, or bread, or pomegranate, or fish. Each step dodged the sounds of merchants selling cloth or pottery or baskets or gold and silver ornaments. Every corner echoed with the noise of animals bahing or braying or brooding; bearing their burden or themselves to be sold within the cacophony that was the marketplace. Three copper drams was all the money the family had until their brother returned late tonight from Caesarea — if he had found work, and if he had found lodging at a fair price. Mother had been very precise in her instructions concerning the use of money. Barley bread and dried fish would be all there would be to eat today and tomorrow. Having made his purchases, Levi walked down the dirt road toward home humming the song that had come alive within him.

As Levi paced along the path, he looked up against the hillside into the azure sky. He saw him. He stopped humming. He stopped walking. He put the basket down and watched for the longest time. Up the hill family after family, one man after another, a few women here and a few women there; all walking after him. Levi was not sure who he was so he asked a man what all the excitement was about. "The master is going to teach," the man said, "Come along boy, come along." They were going toward Sogane. Home was halfway between there and Bethsaida. It would be sort of on his way. "I'll check this master out," said Levi to himself as he picked up the basket. He would listen, but he would also remember the words of the rabbi concerning false prophets.

"I'm gonna beat him so hard that he won't sit down for a week. No," she thought to herself, "that's not long enough. He won't go anywhere until he has recited his school work three times to me. No. Four. He will bring in extra water. He will have to walk with me when I go to the market." While she knew that she would not do all of these things, you could see that behind the anger in her eyes was a dread too deep for words. She looked down the path toward the lake, the path on which Levi should have returned over two hours ago. "Please let him be safe," she said under her breath as she put down the wooden spoon that she held in her hand.

It was at this same side window of the small mud hut that she looked the day the man came. It seemed like yesterday that she saw him coming up the path to tell her of the accident. Jacob and two others killed and many injured when the tower they were working on in Caesarea collapsed. Now young Jacob was working in Caesarea, and Levi was not back. How her life had changed in just a few short years. She would listen to an explanation. No, she would just let him know of her displeasure and fear at his delay. No. If she made up her mind now she knew that she would do the opposite when he arrived.

Levi sat enraptured by this teacher. Never, never ever had he heard the will of God put so beautifully, so simply. He could understand every word, yet he could see that the adults were also hanging on his every word. Levi assumed that there was something more meaningful, an even deeper level of understanding within the words that he took in so readily. The message of this teacher seemed to clear, so wonderful, so marvelous. God had always been so far away, but this rabbi taught that God was as close as your own father. Even though Levi's father was dead, he knew what this rabbi meant. As he listened it was as though all the pain and hurt from his father's death and his brother's absence had been lifted from his heart and mind. Lifted, no not quite, he still mourned the loss of his father, but he found a peace which was a blessing to him.

All the time he was listening, Levi moved up further and further, closer and closer toward the teacher. By this time there were thousands of people and he was so short. He and his basket kept moving and moving and moving.

It was almost dark, and when she heard someone on the path, she sprang from her mat and went to the doorway. She grabbed the wooden spoon as she passed the table. Looking south toward the lake she saw no one. Turning north she saw young Jacob coming down the hillside path from Selucia.

"Oh, Jacob, your brother is missing. I don't know where to turn. I sent him to the market this morning. He should have been home hours ago. I've been up and down the paths, half way to the lake. I don't know what to do."

"I don't know either, mother." The distance in Jacob's voice made Caesarea sound close. "I only have a denarius to bring you. They charged incredible rates for lodging. I have not eaten since breakfast yesterday. There was another accident — six more killed. Maybe I'll be able to find better work next week. I'm too young, I can't do some of the jobs. They won't let me do some of the better jobs. The foreman is superstitious and since Papa died, they won't put me ... I don't know. Is there anything to eat?"

"Your brother is missing. He has been missing since this morning. I don't know where he is. Aren't you listening? Don't you care?"

"Mom, I care. It's dark, we don't know where to begin. There's nothing I can do!"

She turned away wishing Jacob was still alive to hold her; to help her through the trauma of this night.

Levi hummed a psalm as he sat on the tree stump overlooking the house. He stared at the light coming from the window for what seemed to be forever. All of a sudden he knew, at an even deeper level, what the master had meant by the dead burying their own dead and that it was easier to begin a totally new life than to walk back into an old one. He was living life anew. He didn't know how to explain this newness to his mom; how it felt, what it was like. Neither did he know how he was going to explain what happened to the food and the basket. He had gotten into that innocently enough. The master had been talking about how to receive. That if you were to receive anything you must give it: love, forgiveness, respect, understanding, even hope. All these concepts were easy to believe. Then the master began to say that money was the same and food was the same. Levi and his family needed food and money, so if he were to believe he would have to give these fish and this bread. He saw Phillip who used to fish out of Bethsaida. Levi gave him the basket. Phillip passed it on, the next passed it on, the next and the next until it had been emptied out in front of the master. Prayers were said, the bread and fish were passed, and everyone started to eat. They ate and they ate and they ate and the next time he saw the basket it was full and he was too. And that's why he was sitting on that stump. He didn't know whether it would be easier to explain this idea of new life in the spirit; or to explain what had happened to the bread.

She was still crying when she heard him call from the path that he was coming. She stood at the door with her spoon in her hand not knowing whether to hug him or spank him first.

"I know how late I am, and I want to explain everything that has happened today." He held the basket close to him.

"Fine," Mother said in a normal stern voice. "You may explain while your brother eats. I see that you have already eaten."

"I didn't want to start there." He had arranged the basket so that a large piece of bread stuck out from under the cloth. It kind of gave the impression that everything was okay, except that the end of the large piece had been broken off.

"What do you mean, you 'don't want to start there?' "

"I met the Messiah today."

"Blasphemer, young man, I never want to hear you say that again. Do you understand me?"

"I mean I guess he was. I don't know ... all I know is that he talked about God and loving and caring and all the pain I've held inside came out and he took it away. I knew it would come back, but when I concentrated on what he was saying I didn't feel the hurt anymore." Levi went on to explain what happened and what he had heard. Finally he told what had happened to the bread and fish.

When he was finished Mother said, "First, the priests will tell us when the Messiah comes. Second, since you have eaten, you may go to the roof and sweep it and then go to sleep. Third, you are never to go to the market again or mention this so-called Messiah again. Now give me that basket.

"Oh, Jacob! I don't know what to do with that boy," she emptied the two fish and five barley loaves onto the table. "He tells such tales since his father died."

Order Of Service
Lent 3

Opening Words:
> L: Let us worship our Creator, the God of Love.
> **P: God continually preserves and sustains us.**
> L: We have been blessed with an everlasting blessing.
> **P: Through Jesus Christ we have received grace and the blessing of being God's children.**

Hymn: "I've Found A Friend"

Prayer Of Confession: *(Unison)*
> We turn from you, O God, when you ask of us the commitment of time, the commitment of talent, the commitment of money. We center our lives upon ourselves. We fall very short of emulating your love. We ask for return, we seek vengeance, we allow suffering, we permit racism, we sanction injustice, we plead ignorance, we stand silent before the powers who must hear the good news. Give us strength to begin again. Allow us to walk with thee, O Christ. Amen.

Assurance Of Pardon:
> Cease to do evil; learn to do well. Seek judgment, relieve the oppressed, judge the fatherless, plead for the widow. Come now, let us reason together says the Lord: Though your sins be as scarlet, they shall be white as snow ... He has shown thee, O man what is good; what does the Lord require of thee but to do justly, to love mercy, and to walk humbly with thy God ... Live as forgiven people.

Readings: Psalm 107:1-9, 43; Luke 19:1-10

Hymn: "Abide With Me" stanzas 1, 2

Meditation: Zacchaeus

Hymn: "Abide With Me" stanzas 3, 4

Call To Communion:
>L: Let us affirm our faith.
>
>**P: Despite our claims that we could not help it, and that we are not "responsible," we know that each day we have the opportunity to crucify or acquit Jesus. We believe that he continues to suffer and die when we keep others from spiritual growth, convincing them in a hundred subtle ways that they are less worthy of being called sons and daughters of righteousness, children of Abraham. We believe that Christ's resurrection can occur in our life and in the lives around us when we make a choice to affirm God's gift in us. We believe that God grants us each opportunities to serve and to affirm our belief.**
>
>L: Lift up your hearts.
>
>**P: We lift them up to the Lord.**
>
>L: Let us give thanks to the Lord our God.
>
>**P: It is right and good that we give thanks.**

Prayers For Bread And Cup

The Distribution

Dismissal:
>L: Each of us can grow on the inside, dedicating ourselves to spiritual growth. Decide today to grow in love and understanding.
>
>**P: As Christ gives us strength we shall walk with him.**
>
>L: Go in peace, knowing that each person you meet is a child of God.
>
>**P: May the Spirit lead us in joy. Amen.**

Zacchaeus
Lent 3

My Dear Friend:

I am writing you today to tell you of a rather strange happening to our mutual acquaintance Zacchaeus. Since our history of sharing things together goes way back to our childhood, there was no one else with whom I could share this event and somehow make sense of it.

You remember how we used to call him Half-pac-Zac and how he would go absolutely crazy about that, and all the other things we used to do to him? He was so short and he always looked to us for acceptance (which of course we never gave him) and I guess I always felt partly to blame that he became so harsh and bitter from the way we treated him. It was no surprise to any of us, really, when he took the tax office and began wheeling and dealing at the behest of our grand Tetrarch and Governor Pilate to extort extra taxes from the people (including us) and making himself quite rich in the process. I am trying to remember if this was before you moved or after. It seems like forever since you and your family moved back to the land of your father's people. I still miss those great games we used to play, the quiet walks we took to talk, trying to remember and forget. 'Most everyone has moved away. Gone to the city to find work. The only one left of the "crowd" is, you guessed it, Half-pac. Watching him makes me even lonelier. Anyway, we heard that this Nazarene Rabbi, Jesus, was on his way toward Jerusalem and the whole town turned out to see him and maybe have him bless us, or something — I guess I was just curious, I don't know — anyway, we're gathered on the sides of the street and it is like "instant parade," you know? And I'm watching, and I'm watching, and I catch sight of this head popping up and down, up and down. It's Zac, trying to find a place to see the parade. But he can't find a place, and the Rabbi is getting closer and closer. The Rabbi's guys are watchin', I'm watchin', everybody's watchin' 'cept the Zac. Well, there is this sycamore 20, 30 yards down the street. Belongs to Bennie, and he hasn't gotten any more agreeable since you left. So, Zac runs up this tree and leans way out to catch a glimpse of this Rabbi. Bennie took a stick and started hitting Zac on the feet, yelling, "I just pruned that tree, you're gonna break the limbs, get off the tree you short so and so." Well, Zac yells back, "I'm gonna take this tree and your house for back taxes."

"Oh yeah," yells Bennie, "my taxes is paid, no thanks to you."

"Well taxes just doubled," Zac yells back.

Just about this time the Rabbi comes up in front of the tree and I see one of his men whisper something into the Rabbi's ear. The Rabbi stops. The parade stops. We stop. The shouting stops. Everything stops. The Rabbi looks Bennie off and then looking up into the tree calls the "half-pac" by name. "Zacchaeus," he said in a strong and unmistakable voice, "come down from that tree; I would like to take refreshment at your house today."

Wow! That blew everyone away. Everyone's mouth was hanging open. The whole town is whispering, "Why does he want to go there?" and "Does Zacchaeus know this Rabbi?" and "Can this guy really be a Rabbi and know Zacchaeus?" The Pharisees started writing down everything that happened; our Rabbi had this "I thought that Rabbis were supposed to lunch together" look on his face, and everyone just stood there while Zac led Jesus to his house.

They were in there for the longest time, when Marcie, Zac's serving girl came out to tell us what happened. Well, you know that that woman's half crazy, but she said that Zacchaeus was going to give his money away. She said that he had told Jesus that if he had cheated anyone he was going to pay them back fourfold! That was pretty exciting news. So we formed a line.

We stood there for a while and pretty soon Zac and Jesus and his men came out and sure enough crazy Marcie was right. The Zac made this announcement, just like Marcie said, and then sat down at a table and called for his books and he called for money bags and he began the give away. Then things really started to happen.

We all assumed that as soon as Jesus left that the give away would stop, so the big strong guys like me pushed to the front. But I was wrong! Jesus and his men left — I mean he didn't even leave one of his guys there to make sure — they left and Zac kept calling for more money bags.

I'm almost ashamed to tell you this part, but I have to. When it came to be my turn I told Zacchaeus that I think that he cheated me out of 20 shekels. He's looking into his books and can see that I'm lying, but he gives me 2 talents. Two hundred shekels when even with this crazy thing going on he shouldn't have given me more than 80.

"No Zac," I said, a flush of guilt coming all over me. "I made a mistake, it wasn't 20, you . . . you, you don't owe me this much.'

"Jake," he said, "I owe you at least this much for hating you all these years."

I stammered. "It's I that should pay you."

"No," was his response. "Next."

I wanted to be mad, for I realized that it was the way I treated him that has caused his hate for me. I wanted to explode with indignation at his generosity, at his patronizing my sin. I wanted to cry and hug him and take back 30 years of name calling and snubbing that made this man feel smaller than he was physically. But most of all I wanted to find out what that Rabbi had said that made such a difference in Zacchaeus. I had to know what made that man whose love had been stunted, grow in such a short time.

But I could hear the crowd behind me, Bennie swearing up and down, wanting four new trees for a nick in one sycamore. And I didn't know what to do, so I sat down and waited. Waited while a small man gave away a large fortune and became a giant.

I saw him count to a Pharisee; give compassionately to a widow; explain knowingly to a fisherman; and finally when it was over give a sigh of relief and a cry of exaltation. I asked him to sit with me and tell me what the Rabbi told him.

"Well, I don't know," he began in a tone and voice that I had not heard from him for a long time. "But do you remember old Rabbi Zolts?"

I nodded.

"Do you remember those dumb little sayings he used to give us?"

I nodded again, remembering.

"Well, Jesus reminded me of one of them, 'That a man never stands so tall as when he kneels to God in prayer.' I could hear old Zolts, God grant him peace, saying that one."

"Well, if you are never so tall as when you kneel, I guess that I'm closer to God than you are."

That struck me kind of funny, and I started to laugh. And we laughed and laughed until we cried.

"Jesus reminds you of Rabbi Zolts?" I continued to laugh.

"Yes, well, no, of course not. What he said was that it's not what's on the outside but what is on the inside that counts. You only have to be tall on the inside. He called me a Son of Abraham. I was sure, all my life, that you had to be big and tall and handsome to be a Son of Abraham. And I never thought that I was going to make it, so I quit trying. But you only have to be tall on the inside because that is where the real growth takes place. In faith, in understanding, in hope and love. Those are the real things that matter in your life. That's where real growth takes place. And Jesus made me commit myself to that kind of growth."

In order for him to keep his commitment the first thing that had to go was greed and guilt. Jesus and Zacchaeus agreed that this would be proper penance. Zacchaeus is a changed man. I wish that I could change also. I have decided that I too will make a commitment to growth. I am going to

Jerusalem for Passover this year and try to find this Jesus. And maybe I will even find myself.

Simon, why don't you come to Jerusalem this Passover. Cyrenaica is a long trip, but please try to come. Let's find Jesus together.

Your friend,

Jacob

Order Of Service
Lent 4

Opening Words:
   L: Let us worship our Creator, the God of Love.
   P: God continually preserves and sustains us.
   L: We have been loved with an everlasting love.
   P: Through Jesus Christ we have been given complete knowledge of God's glory.

Hymn: "Are Ye Able"

Prayer Of Confession: *(Unison)*
   Have mercy upon me, O God, according to thy loving kindness. According unto thy tender mercies blot out my transgressions. Wash me thoroughly from my iniquity, and cleanse me from my sin. I acknowledge my transgressions; my sin is ever before me. Against thee, only have I sinned. Cast me not from thy presence; take not thy Holy Spirit from me. Restore me to the joy of thy salvation, and uphold me with thy spirit.

Assurance Of Pardon:
   May the Lord open our lips and our mouths to show forth praise due God's holy name. The Lord does not desire sacrifices and burnt offerings. A broken and contrite heart is not despised by God.

Readings: Joel 2:12-19; Luke 13:18-22

Hymn: "O Love That Will Not Let Me Go" stanzas 1, 2

Meditation: The Ring

Hymn: "O Love That Will Not Let Me Go" stanzas 3, 4

Call To Communion:

L: Let us affirm our faith.

P: **We search for a way in this world and find God's redeeming love in the most unlikely places. As Jesus taught in towns and villages on his way to Jerusalem many heard but many remained unconvinced. We believe that it is our task to continue to teach as Jesus taught, helping the world find reconciliation in the love of God which is in Christ Jesus.**

L: Lift up your hearts.

P: **We lift them up unto the Lord.**

L: Let us give thanks to the Lord our God.

P: **It is right and good that we give thanks.**

Prayers For Bread And Cup

The Distribution

Dismissal:

L: Now may the love of God rule us,

P: **The light of God guide us,**

L: The wisdom of God preserve us,

P: **The presence of God watch over us.**

L: May we find hope in the peace of God that transcends and understands all things.

The Ring
Lent 4

It was not so much the value of the ring, although very likely it was the most precious possession the family had in both the monetary and sentimental senses of the word. It was that she had been told over and over again not to play with the precious things which mother kept in the small wooden box in the bottom of the dowry chest. Because of this loss the family felt none of the usual joy of the walk to Emmatha on their weekly journey to Synagogue. During the quarter mile walk to the village, Father generally asked the children questions about the Torah and there was always a discussion about the points and precepts of the Law. While some of the fun of this weekly discussion had been lost recently (Stephen, having reached his Bar Mitzvah) the family would ask and answer questions pushing point after point until Father would tell a midrash settling the issue. But today there was no discussion. Today it seemed that all life and faith had lost its meaning. Today there was an impatient silence as Father waited for Stephen to begin his question. Today Sarah and Mother walked patiently along, listening but not hearing. Today faith and the Law were the domain of silent men.

Perhaps it was because Sarah felt so badly about the ring that she felt as if one of Father's questions and every one of Stephen's eventual answers were directed at her.

"It's not my fault," she cried, holding back the tears. "I'm sorry that I was playing with the ring. I didn't steal it. I didn't really lose it. I just don't know where it is. It's just missing. I'm sorry."

"We know you're sorry. You said you're sorry; you should be sorry. Now, please drop it." Mother's voice sounded bitter, but not as harsh as when the loss was first noticed Wednesday.

"Every time you talk about it, simply reminds me of how much grandmother's ring meant to me."

The silence of the rest of their walk betrayed the anger and yes, the sense of grief the whole family felt this Sabbath day.

As Father and Stephen entered the synagogue, Mother watched as the two blended in with the other men in prayer shawls. She heard the song and the scriptures being read.

"Well, Sarah, let's walk over to the well and hear the news of the day. Sarah ..."

While she did not see the girl go, Mother assumed that since they usually went to the well, Sarah had simply gone ahead. When she entered the square, however, she still did not see her, in fact her dismay gave way to shock for the plaza was virtually deserted. A commotion could be heard on a side street which distracted her from the searching glance she had cast upon the square.

As she turned to see from where the noise had come, she saw Sarah's dress (she thought) slip into the side street in the direction of the sound.

"Men of Emmatha and the Decapolis," began the Rabbi in his address to the men gathered for Sabbath service, "we must be wary of those who claim to teach the law but do not follow it. There is one, currently, who has taken extreme liberties with the law. We believe, also, that he may be guilty of blasphemy." The Rabbi went on to explain to the men that major disruptions had occurred in most of the cities on the east side of Galilee. While the itinerant had been making most of the trouble in larger towns such as Capernaum, he was said to have close personal friends as near as Bethsaida. It had been reported recently that he and his followers were now stopping in small towns and making friends, as usual, with tax collectors and publicans, and casting a strange influence on women and children who had no appreciation for the law of God, and had no way of discriminating between debate and error.

"We must take care," he continued, "to keep our loved ones from the influence of these teachings to be sure. But we must also be very precise in our accusations against this charlatan, and make documentation as prescribed so that we may take lawful action against this heretic. God's word is clear. Eating with those unclean, eating with hands unclean, both bring the response of condemnation from the God of Abraham, Isaac, and Jacob. The scripture teaches and confirms: we must be pure."

"He is in our town now!" a voice burst into the synagogue. "He is just off the square. We must stop him from blaspheming in front of our wives and children."

It was as if King David himself called for an army to fend off the Philistines. As if with one body the men arose. As if with one voice they cried, "death to the blasphemer." Gideon, seeking to fight the Midianites could not have found such a noble and devoted army. Raising his hand above his head as he went through the door, the Rabbi led the men from the synagogue into the hot sun. Down the street, onto the square, into the side street where the publicans and harlots entertained themselves in debauchery.

Those gathered on the side street in Emmatha watched as an itinerant preacher spoke about counting the cost of following the Word of God. People from the crowd reached out to him. He healed them. Sarah watched as a blind man could see. Oh, the joy of finding sight. A cripple began to walk. What joy in finding that you could walk after being lame. Sarah wondered if the hurt which she felt inside her could be easily fixed or healed as this wonderful man could cure these physical problems. She wanted to know if there were some miracle to help her find the lost ring. Some way he could help her remember. You would have to be brave to walk right up to someone like that. More than anything else today, Sarah felt too lonely and scared inside to be that brave. Just as she said to herself, "maybe he could whisper the exact place" she heard the shouts of the men approaching.

"Father," said Sarah interrupting an otherwise silent walk home, "what did that Rabbi mean when he talked about the people finding what they had lost. That God was happy when people sin, or just happy when they repent, and turn to God again?"

Father did not answer the question. His gallant army had backed down in the confrontation with the Nazarene. The story of the woman and the coin he had heard before, but the midrash of the sheep being linked with the story of the lost son was new and took the whole company by surprise. The Nazarene had tricked them. Instead of countering shout with shout, force with force — although who knows how many daggers were concealed within the robes of these filthy publicans and those thieving harlots — he sat, speaking softly and slowly. He tenderly captured the wives and children whom they had come to save.

"God is happy when we follow the law," Father finally said. He thought, "It is not right, it was as if the son who squandered the Father's fortune was the hero of the story. The Father was much too willing to take the squanderer back as if nothing happened. Overly generous. That is not the law. That is weakness. If a god were moved by tears or by heathen ritual, what is the difference. How can a weak God be the strength of Israel?"

"Mother," Sarah asked, "the woman who found the coin and had a party; would she not have spent more on the party than on the coin?"

"I guess what the Rabbi meant ..."

"He is not a Rabbi," Father's voice interrupted, breaking Mother's thought.

"I guess what the Nazarene meant was that the joy in finding something is often worth more than what had actually been lost."

Sarah, obviously confused by the events of the day again asked, "If happiness is more important than actually finding the thing we have lost, how come I can't get over the missing ring?"

"Oh Sarah, there are things we find within ourselves which God has given us. Abilities. Love for the law. Through the law we have a sense of justice and righteousness. We have a view of hope. The man who divided his money lost a portion of his estate, but he found a son who would be willing to stay with him and expect nothing more than to be a servant. The best part of life is not in the getting, but in being able to give. That is why I have been so upset. I wanted to feel the pride and joy of giving just as my mother proudly gave that ring to me. It was part of who I am, who I was. Now I cannot give you the only thing that was mine to give."

"Oh Mother, you have given me so much." Sarah was crying, but with different tears this time. "You are teaching me how to be a good wife. To be a wife as the Book of Proverbs describes. You taught me how to sew, how to weave, how to cook and bake. You have given me so much more than this one thing which was lost. Giving is one of the things that you taught me."

Daughter hugged Mother. Mother hugged daughter. They continued their walk toward home.

Sarah looked at her mother. "Before this whole thing happened," she said, "I so enjoyed the time we spent together Wednesday making bread. Some for ourselves; some for the widow. You wanted to show me how to knead the bread. As I smoothed the top of the cup of flour, I looked at my hand and said to myself, 'Sarah, you had better take off' ... yes! The ring. I took it off when I was measuring the flour. It dropped in the flour. I'm sure of it."

"Who would have thought to look in the flour?" said Mother as she ran toward home.

"I think it's in the flour!" yelled Sarah to Father and Stephen as she too began to run the hundred yards to the house. Father and Stephen and Sarah arrived at the house at the same time. The door was ajar. They opened the door fully and as they went inside they could see the dark outline of Mother in the cloud of white dust enveloping the table. Her hair was white, her dress was white. Her arms were white as snow.

"Did you find it?"

Order Of Service
Lent 5

Opening Words:
>L: Let us worship our Creator, the God of Love.
>
>**P: God continually preserves and sustains us.**
>
>L: We have been forgiven with an all embracing acceptance.
>
>**P: Through Jesus Christ we have received the full love of God.**

Hymn: "Jesus, The Very Thought Of Thee"

Prayer Of Confession: *(Unison)*
   O God of all people and places, you are present within this room, within our lives, within our hearts. But we are self-centered, seeking our own way, claiming and clinging to things as if they were more important than that which you give. While we seek to live at peace with all, O Lord, we often fail to stand up for what is just and right. Help us, Lord, to believe that your presence makes our gifts worthy, and our lives living sacrifices unto you. Forgive us, in Jesus' name. Amen.

Assurance Of Pardon:
   Each day we are challenged to obey God in a way that is deeper and more profound than the previous day. God gives us strength to approach each day as a new day and trusts us to live that day as a gift to Christ. Friends, hear the good news of God: In Jesus Christ we are forgiven.

Readings: Psalm 36:5-9; Luke 21:1-4

Hymn: "Love Divine, All Loves Excelling" stanzas 1, 2

Meditation: A Penny's Worth Of Thanks

Hymn: "Love Divine, All Loves Excelling" stanzas 3, 4

Call To Communion:
  L: Let us affirm our faith.
  P: We believe that each person is given a special blessing to be shared for the upbuilding of the community of faith. Each person affirms that gift in the power of the Holy Spirit. Whether we are poor or rich we are to give our all to God, with those who have received more giving more. We believe that unless our hearts are on fire with thanksgiving that our gifts are hollow, not hallowed.
  L: Lift up your hearts.
  P: We lift them up to the Lord.
  L: Let us give thanks to the Lord our God.
  P: It is good and right that we do this.

Prayers For Bread And Cup

The Distribution

Dismissal:
  L: Let us go forth in thanksgiving, remembering that all good gifts come from the Lord, Our God.
  P: Let us rejoice and bear witness to God's love.
  L: Go in peace.
  P: May the Spirit lead us in joy. Amen.

A Penny's Worth Of Thanks
Lent 5

Matilda Rosencrantz was an old woman who lived long ago. To all appearances she had only life and breath for which to be thankful. She had never been what you would call "attractive," and the ravages of time and widowhood had taken their toll on her countenance. The single tooth that she had in her mouth protruded when she smiled, and when she frowned, and when she just sat and stared at the walls of her small home, in which she sat most of the time when not out trying to sell flowers, or out gleaning the fields for grain to make porridge and bread. The small house in which she lived was more than adequate for her needs, however, and quite a generous gift from her third cousin (twice removed), who often told her, "I could get a hundred easy for this house, if I weren't so generous by letting you live here."

She arose from her one chair to answer the knocking at her door. It was Malcolm, her third cousin (twice removed) who greeted her by saying, "The Rabbi said that we men of means should make sure that our relatives are well cared for over the holiday season. So after temple tomorrow come over to the house and I'll give you some cheese and meat and stuff. Okay?"

Matilda thought that this was an extremely kind gesture on her cousin's part (especially being third and twice removed). After thanking him for the invitation, she left the house immediately for the hills outside the city to find and bundle some lovely wild flowers to sell so that she might buy a small thank you gift for him as repayment for his generosity.

As she picked the wild flowers growing on the hillside, she thanked God for the many blessings bestowed on her. For her life and breath. For her family, mostly now departed, and for the many wonderful times they shared together in days gone by. She thanked God for the children playing below her in the stream, for, although she and her husband were not blessed with children, she so enjoyed watching their enthusiasm for life. She thanked God for the wonderful weather on the day, for the warmth of the sun, the light and gentle breeze; she thanked God for the rain of the week before, which had helped the flowers grow. She even thanked God for the ragged and tattered old basket in which she so gently placed the flowers to bundle.

God had indeed been good to her, she thought. It had only taken five hours to pick and sell the 15 carefully bundled bouquets: "A ha'penny each or three bunches for a penny." As she went back to her home she stopped at the market to buy some rice and bread (it would go well with the meat); she gave a half cent to a beggar with one leg (poor thing); a package of lamp wicks for Malcolm (she had to make sure that they were the new kind, the Roman kind, for Malcolm had all the latest things). Finally, she kept some money for the offering at temple (it felt good to be able to give again). Several times she had pretended to drop coins into the offering, but knew that mouths turned to whisper in eager ears at the silence of the sound. She had been caught in the drama of her poverty.

Arriving home, she cooked some rice, ate some bread, and rolled out her bed. She thanked God that she had been part of a beautiful day, and that she would have bread for tomorrow.

The morning found her up and present at the temple, standing with the others who had something to offer at the service. There was a space between her and the man in front of her. He kept nudging forward to the man in front of him. That was okay, she did not want to get dust from her floor on his fine shoes. She waited in anticipation for the priests to begin their liturgy, the Rabbi to read the words of scripture, and the men of the chorus to lead the Psalm. What she clutched in her hand represented all that she had and all that she was. She saw Malcolm. He was talking to the influential people.

There were soldiers and guards in various places. She saw that the new Rabbi was over on the steps. Some of his followers were with him. Malcolm did not like him. Well, he did not like any of them for that matter. He said that this Rabbi was a troublemaker; said that he was too, something; said that they'd probably get rid of him. He said he just wasn't a good Rabbi, "you know." Matilda really didn't know. She really liked him. Thought he spoke really well. Enjoyed his stories. But, they had had trouble before, with other Rabbis. Who was she to make waves. She smiled at him.

Oh! It was her turn. She dropped two copper coins amounting to a penny. She hoped it would turn out all right for the new Rabbi. She wondered what he thought. He knew that she was poor.

> *"And calling his disciples to him, Jesus said to them, 'Truly I say to you, this poor widow put in more than all the contributors to the treasury: for they all put in out of their surplus, but she out of her poverty, put in all she owned, all she had to live on.' "*

Order Of Service
Palm Sunday (Or Maundy Thursday)

Opening Words:
    L: Let us worship God, our creator and redeemer, the God of Love.

    P: God continually preserves and sustains us.

    L: We have been forgiven with a powerful and engaging love.

    P: Christ has entered into our hearts and lives, waiting for us to recognize his Lordship over us.

Hymn: "All Glory Laud And Honor"

Prayer Of Confession: *(Unison)*
    Our hearts break, O Lord, as we watch the poverty and loneliness that confront us on the street and in the news: we feel powerless to respond. We are not certain of what to do. We cry out, but words do not form in our mouths. Free us to act in thy name, O Lord. Free us to respond to your world in need. Let us be assured that the acts of searching for our true selves do matter in this world. Assure us that small acts of kindness done in the name of Christ influence people more than we know. Fill us with thy spirit, O great God, as we sing Hosanna to the one who is to come. Amen.

Assurance Of Pardon:
    Blessed is the one who comes in the name of the Lord. In our study, in our observance of religious tradition, in our acts of conscience and conviction we seek to stand with those who stand to be counted as a follower of Christ. We are assured that we shall never be put to shame. We are assured that we shall receive justice from a compassionate God. We are assured that if we confess Christ before others, he shall confess us before the God of Heaven and earth. Live as forgiven people.

Hymn: "O Master Let Me Walk With Thee" stanzas 1, 2

Meditation: The Water Boy

Hymn: "O Master Let Me Walk With Thee" stanzas 3, 4

Service Of The Lord's Supper:
- L: Let us affirm our faith.
- **P: We believe that God's love came to us in the flesh as Jesus of Nazareth. We believe that he was the suffering servant of whom the prophet Isaiah spoke centuries ago. We believe that all must seek to know the story of Christ. We believe that it is part of our mission to share that story. We believe that there is much to learn from suffering and that God will stand with us in the midst of our pain, our growing, our rejection, and our searching.**
- L: Lift up your hearts.
- **P: We lift them up to the Lord.**
- L: Let us give thanks to the Lord our God.
- **P: It is right and good that we give thanks and praise.**

Prayers For Bread And Cup

The Distribution

Dismissal:
- L: There are times when we wish we could serve God more than we do, but our pride gets in the way. There are times when we have done the wrong thing. Trusting God means to work out your salvation in fear and trembling.
- **P: Christ gives us guidance in our search for belonging.**
- L: Go in peace, knowing that true inner peace comes from serving Christ.
- **P: May the Spirit of God lead us in joy.**

The Water Boy
palm Sunday (OR maundy thursday)

"This is the pits," John said as he picked up the terra cotta water jug and walked toward the doorway. "I bet I'll be the only man at the fountain." He paused. "And I'm not going to carry it on my head!"

"John, you will not be the only boy," Mother caught herself. "Excuse me, young man who has to pick up the extra chores as the Passover approaches, I am sure that you will see several of your friends on your way to the fountain, and they will be cleaning or hauling or helping ready their families' Passover rooms for the pilgrims gathering for the holy days. The next five days will go fast. Now please go, help."

John held the water jar under his left arm and opened the door and peeked out into the street. "So far, so good," he thought to himself, "I guess I can do this for five days."

He stepped out onto the street, water jar half hidden between his robe and his tunic. The robe was his father's, hemmed for John on the occasion of his Bar Mitzvah (a rabbinic ceremony that celebrated becoming a man). Boys only wore tunics and coats, and while it was not an official symbol, the robe, striped and flowing, did two things. First, it announced to the world that here was a man of Israel coming down the street. Second, it kept people from noticing that he was carrying a water jar. From behind you couldn't see it and from the front, well, he would just have to be sharp.

Walking up the street he noticed the robe of old Mandrel; in it was his friend Mordecai. Was Mother right? Was he, too, doing women's chores? Doubt lingered. Should he chance conversation? Ah, slow down, John thought to himself, here is a corner. If things get tight, I can bail out by turning left and circling around to the fountain.

"Mort, Mort," John at first squeaked and then said in a deeper tone. "What are you up to today?"

The corner trick worked, but it was Mordecai who took advantage of it. A head peeked back around the corner of the building.

"Oh, John, is that you! I had already started to turn when I heard ..." his eyes caught the water jar and the smile erupted across his whole face. "Going for water?"

"Yes."

"Well, I've got to be going," said Mort beating a hasty retreat.

"Get out of here," John called to his friend, figuring that at least he may be able to turn this one calamity into a lookout against the next one. "Come on, help me out!"

John reached around the corner for Mandrel's robe to grab Mort. What he held in his hand, however was a tablecloth and a couch sheet.

"Mom was right," John yelled, "You are out doing chores, too."

"Give me those sheets," Mordecai had lost his smile. "I'm just ..."

"You're just doing the same thing that I am. Helping to get ready for Passover."

"Don't tell," said Mort, almost pleading.

"Who me?" John shot back, gripping the water jar with his right hand and pulling it two or three inches out of the robe then stuffing it back.

The two boys, excuse me, young men walked toward the plaza where the fountain and the laundry were both located. They discussed how the Bar Mitzvah had changed their opinion of who they were and how they viewed life. Last year they did these same chores as "boys" and it did not bother either of them. "But when I am a man, I put away childish things," they quoted from the teachings of the Pharisaic Rabbi, Gamaliel.

It is a terrible thing, this 13th year of life. Hormones are God's best and worst invention. Sometimes best and worst follow each other by a day. Sometimes by the hour. Sometimes by the minute. Today was no exception. The serious discussion about manhood and the observance of the teachings was interrupted by Mort's sudden command, "Stop!"

"It's Esther," John yelled. "Let's get out of here."

But there was no place to turn.

John's father and Esther's father went to the cafe last week. He shuddered to think what that might mean. John could tell that Esther had had "the talk" with her mom. There were three talks really. He overheard his mom giving part of "the talk" to his sister. Part one was "embarrassing men by simply existing." Esther had this part down pat.

"Hi John," said Esther, "helping today?"

"Yeah, my mom needs this so full that she couldn't carry it. Let's go, Mort." They ran down a side street that lead, well — away from Esther. Turning the corner they plastered themselves against the wall of the house, bundles and jar in hand.

"Hosanna! Hosanna!" A crowd of people gathered to watch a small parade. "Blessed is he that comes in the name of the Lord! Hosanna in the highest."

"Do you know who that is?" Mort gasped. "That's the Nazarene Rabbi that was in Bethany yesterday. My dad said that this Rabbi brought this dead guy out of the tomb and that he's alive!"

"Get outta here."

"I'm serious ..."

"Take off your robe, young men of Israel," a voice confronted them from within the crowd, "and allow the Master to ride over it. Meet your Messiah. Receive his blessing of life ..."

"O man, let's get outta here!" John and Mort said at the same time. They ran back up the alley, figuring that Esther and hormones were safer and more certain than this. They ran into the plaza — John to the fountain, Mort to the laundry. After transacting their business, the two carried the water jar as quickly as they could down the street. They entered John's house and slammed the door. "Mother, Father." No one was home. They were safe. I guess.

Later that night the family sat after dinner to discuss the day. Father told about his day and about a most incredible event at the temple. He had stopped by to offer a sacrifice. He had money today, and later in the week he hoped he would be hosting a Seder and be unable to get away.

"Well, said Father, "I was waiting at a change table to get shekels and this guy comes in yelling about 'The Father's house. I'll tear down this temple and rebuild it in three days.' He started to turn over tables, breaking pigeon cages, scattering grain and sheep and, it was a mess. He had a whip and everything! I've never seen anything like it."

"Was that the Nazarene Rabbi?"

"Yes," said Father, "I don't know what this world's coming to."

"I saw him today in a parade. Mort said that some rich guy in Bethany came back to life when this Rabbi called him."

"I heard about that," Mother said. "I heard him speak in the courtyard when I was passing by. I think that he has some good points — especially about those temple money-changers."

"We've been through this before," Father said. "To live in the community of the faith we must offer to God acceptable offerings, as prescribed by the law. Where would we grow grain in the city? Where would we graze sheep? On top of the roof? I get paid for my work in Roman coin, I would not dishonor God by giving a coin with Caesar's head on it. So we exchange the money."

"Mort and I were thinking about getting some pigeons. You know if they're well trained, you can make some good money . . ."

"John, please, we aren't talking about private enterprise, we are talking about purchasing guilt and sin offerings," Father said.

"The dill and timon from my kitchen herb garden are the only true tithing that we do. You have to buy everything else."

"Of course I do, I cut stone for a living. I don't grow crops. But people who live in the city shouldn't have different rules than farmers. There is only one Torah, but there are several parts. There is only one vocation for a Jew. But there are several occupations. My skill has crafted this spacious home. We host pilgrims. We tithe from your garden, and from all our income. But I don't grow grain. I don't raise sheep. This is the only way it works."

"No. There has to be a better way. Those who bring livestock and grain don't need shekels. For us it is a tax, not an offering. What you do and who you are must be given to God without the need of money changing. If the Herodians cannot accept you and who and what you are then the temple has lost touch with the people."

While it is the men who speak of the household of faith of Israel, it is often the women who close the discussions about running the house.

As the day of the Passover approached, carrying the water jar was easier and easier for John. He and Mort and some of the others took all the extra chores in stride and on occasion John even tried carrying it on his head. The dinner discussions, however, were harder and harder on John's parents. Each night Father and Mother saw two sides of the latest event in the life of this Nazarene Rabbi. It is not that Father did not like the Rabbi, but he was afraid of what might happen to him and to his followers. To avoid saying so, he would argue about what the Nazarene really meant.

"If he was a Zealot, well, we know what to do with hot heads. If an Essene, he'd want to be separate, and I'd say 'fine.' If he were a traditionalist he would not be saying what he says."

"You don't like him because you can't classify him," Mother responded.

"No. I do like him. He just doesn't fit. People are like the stones I cut. Each one has a niche into which they fit, with a little shaving here and there. But this one feels like the cornerstone for a new wall. But the temple doesn't need a new wall."

"He will be teaching tomorrow. Let us go together to hear?" Mother asked in a way that Father could not refuse.

The next day, the day of the slaughtering of the lambs, when the family had returned from temple, Mother called John.

"I need you to get some more water for the feast of unleavened bread. Take your time going to the fountain, but don't take any side trips."

"Okay."

About halfway back from the fountain John had this feeling that he was being followed. He casually looked around. None of his friends were around. Everybody looked familiar. Well, no one looked strange, or I should say stranger than anyone else. When he reached the house, a hand came from behind him to help with the door.

"Thanks."

"Is the householder at home? We are seeking a room for the Passover."

John placed the voice. It was the same guy that said the Nazarene Rabbi should ride over his robe.

"I'll get my dad."

Arrangements for the Seder were made. It was like Mother knew these guys, but John did not know how.

"You sent a very good signal," said one of the men.

"I didn't really need the water," Mother replied almost laughing.

John's mood soured. "So she really didn't need the water!" he thought to himself. "It was bad enough to be sent out when it was necessary. Now I'm a messenger boy, a signal."

John brooded about this turn of events all afternoon. He did his chores, but not enthusiastically. He swept the upper room, helped Father arrange the tables. He arranged the Matzo so that it could be easily picked up and ceremoniously broken. Would Father and Mother send him to this room to ask the four questions? Would father delegate the other servants' jobs to him? Would he be a man or a boy forever? He would be a man!

When the guests arrived he was not shocked that it was the Nazarene Rabbi and his followers. There were some younger guys. And Mr. Voice.

"Well," he thought to himself, "I may as well get this over with." And he picked up the basin and pitcher and two towels. "I hate doing this."

He knocked on the door and pushed it open with his back, holding the pitcher and basin in front of him.

"I welcome you to this house," he said in a stolid and prepared manner, "and to prepare you for the feast of Unleavened Bread, I have brought water and basin to remove the dust from your feet from your long sojourn. May you never be considered a stranger here or anywhere in Israel."

As John bent down to place the basin on the floor, it felt as if the towels were slipping from his shoulder. They weren't slipping, the Nazarene Rabbi had them in his hand.

"Sir," the Rabbi looked at John, "will you be so kind as to hold my robe for a moment?"

The Rabbi gave John his robe and tied one towel around his waist and put the other over his shoulder and went to the table with the basin.

Mr. Voice, a fisherman named Peter, said that he would rather do the washing. Then another said he would. The Rabbi silenced them with a glance. "If I do not wash you, you shall not be part of me. I came to serve God, and serving God means being a servant to you."

John watched as each one, in turn, was washed by the Rabbi Jesus. Except for one, all of them were submissive in receiving this gift from their teacher. Just then Father entered with wine and Matzos, Mother followed with the Z'roah of lamb and the bitter root.

"Will you go and get the plates, with the Karpas and egg, and the Dimah?"

"Right away. And Mother?"

"Yes, John Mark?"

"If these travelers need someone to ask the four questions, I would be glad to help them."

Order Of Service
Good Friday

Opening Words:
    L: Let us worship our Creator, the God of Love.

    P: God continually preserves and sustains us.

    L: We have been forgiven with an intimate and involving love.

    P: Through Jesus Christ we have received the full love of God.

Hymn: "In The Cross Of Christ I Glory"

Prayer Of Confession: *(Unison)*
    Holy God, in Christ Jesus you promise a new life. Yet we cling to the old life with its broken form instead of seeking the wholeness of life. We glory not in the death of Christ but in our own achievements. We build walls that separate us and hide behind them. We remember our baptism and are convicted of our sin. Forgive us, we pray, in Jesus' name.

Assurance Of Pardon:
    If we have been united with Christ in a death like his, we shall certainly be united with him in a resurrection like his. In death he died to sin once and for all. In life he lives to God. We must consider ourselves dead to sin and alive to God. Believe the good news: In Christ we are forgiven.

Readings: Psalm 56; Luke 22:54-62

Hymn: "Holy Spirit, Truth Divine" stanzas 1, 2

Meditation: Excuse Me, Do You Know Him?

Hymn: "Holy Spirit, Truth Divine" stanzas 3, 4

Call To Communion:

    L: Let us affirm our faith.

    P: We believe that we are the only Bible that some people will ever know. We believe that if the apostles can fall short of obediently acknowledging Christ, that there is hope for us. We trust that God will give each of us many opportunities to acknowledge Christ and that God will continue to seek and challenge those to whom our witness seems denial.

    L: Lift up your hearts.

    P: We lift them up to the Lord.

    L: Let us give thanks to the Lord our God.

    P: It is right and good that we give thanks and praise.

Prayers For Bread And Cup

The Distribution

Dismissal:

    L: Excuse me, do you know him?

    P: Yes, we acknowledge Jesus as the Christ.

    L: Before the cock crows, you will deny him.

    P: Before the dawn comes, he will forgive us!

    L: Go in peace.

    P: May the Spirit lead us toward joy.

Excuse Me, Did You Know Him?
Good Friday

Moshie Caphar-Saba was a woodcutter. He was not what you would call a professional woodcutter, he just did it for a living. This is to say that his family connections could have seen him in another line of work, but like many others of his generation, he asked for and received his share of the family inheritance, went off to seek his fortune and left the farming to his brothers. The family still carried the old name of the town, Caphar-Saba, even though the Romans re-named and re-built the town as Antipatris some 50 maybe 60 years ago now. It was when his grandfather was young. He remembered his grandfather talking about the legion appearing, the destruction, the bread stolen from the homes, the re-building.

The roots of the family went deep into the soil of the farm, and it was difficult in one sense for Moshie to leave. In another sense, however, to be free from the pettiness of his elder brothers, free from the foolishness of family expectations, free from the hopelessness of those who chose for themselves less than they could have been, rather than to leave the homeplace. These freedoms made life on the road with the legion both exciting and fulfilling. There were occasional pangs of doubt when he would hear of one of his former friends doing well in the trades, but all in all he would not change — well, too much about his life.

Wherever he had followed the legion, even in Antipatris, the market for his services had been okay, but he knew that he would do quite well. Every day more pilgrims came to Jerusalem for the Holy days, and every day more and more legionnaires arrived to keep them in line. He had not meant to go to Jerusalem. He had just followed the legion one day, and Jerusalem is where they went. He had noticed that when you gave the troops a chance to drink some, they would pay quite well for wood for their bivouac fires. Moshie would have a small bundle of wood, take orders, tell them to relax, take his sweet time gathering their orders and then bring the wood and collect.

He had earned the respect of the legionnaires, and he respected them. They were rough. You knew not to cross them. Moshie knew that you must give them what they expect. They expected you to cheat them a little bit, but you had better be good at it. That is where the respect came in.

Moshie was what you might call a semi-observant Jew. He studied the Torah with the Rabbi in Antipatris, but school was never what interested him. It was hard for his father to understand with Moshie's ability to memorize the scripture and his command of the midrash traditions how his son could work for the Romans.

Moshie fully understood that he was working for those occupying his homeland, but what could he do about it? He didn't go in for any of that radical or revolutionary stuff. Zealot, Essene — who needs them. Neither did he care for the party system of the Jews: Pharisee or Sadducee who cares? Moshie Caphar-Saba was in limbo, politically and religiously.

"Maybe that's why I'm struck by this man," he thought to himself as he delivered firewood to the soldiers who were warming themselves in the courtyard. Two things really struck him about the Nazarene.

First, he had been awestruck when Omed was healed. He had been an acquaintance of Omed the blind beggar since moving to Jerusalem. He had been looking for another source of wood and had been out the Jericho Road toward the Wadi Qelt, and there had found a catch of wood from the rainy season. Coming back to town he saw a beggar sitting by the side of the road. After four or five times seeing the beggar, he began to give a piece of wood when he went past. Initially as an act of compassion, then as an act of friendship.

Well, to make a long story short, earlier in the week this Nazarene Rabbi had been coming to Jerusalem and had, by some trick, or magic, or miracle, or something given Omed his sight. Now I know what you're thinking, but he wasn't one of those show guys. Omed was really blind. And when Moshie came back to Jerusalem yesterday, he saw Omed and Omed saw him. Well, he wanted to know what had happened. Omed said it was this Nazarene, and that he was going to begin using his family name again. From now on he was Omed bar Timaeus. Anyway, Moshie was impressed, to say the least, at what had happened to Omed.

The second thing that had Moshie thinking about this Rabbi who had been arrested was that he had some good jabs at the hypocrisy of the big boys at the Sanhedrin. Although several of them had been his friends in the selling trades, when the Nazarene threw the cheaters out of the temple Moshie had a difficult time not laughing out loud. Also, all those fancy lawyers lined up to ask him questions about the Law of Moses. The Rabbi cut them to ribbons with their own words. It was great.

Being in political limbo, Moshie could root for anybody. He thought that this Rabbi was pretty slick, a nice guy, someone you could listen to, and who might even listen to you. That was the difference, he thought. The Pharisees always talked about the rules, and about the temple practices. The rabbis always talked more about God, and this Jesus more personally and more eloquently than any of them.

And so it was that, in the midst of his questioning that Moshie Caphar-Saba, the woodcutter, delivering wood to the sentries' fires in the courtyard of the High Priest Caiaphas, decided that he needed some answers. A little while ago two service girls asked this guy if he had been one of the disciples of the Nazarene. He had told them he was not, but from the accent Moshie could tell that he was definitely a Galilean.

Moshie thought, "Why would someone deny their master? Isn't it a privilege to die for someone or something you believe in?" Maybe not. Maybe he had been hanging around legionnaires too much, and their macabre sense of duty had rubbed off on him. But still, a man ought to have a center, and if you become a disciple of someone, it seems that you ought to stick up for what he says. Either that or find another teacher. While Moshie Caphar-Saba didn't figure himself to be any more curious than any other man, he just had to know if this guy sulking around in the shadows of the dark courtyard could shed any light on this Rabbi, his teachings, and on his friend Omed.

How to approach him? He wanted to find out about Omed. It's not like he wanted to turn the guy in to the authorities or anything, or get him in trouble or anything. He just wanted to know more about Jesus: what he taught, why he had been arrested, and maybe why this guy wouldn't stick up for his master.

Moshie picked up his bundle of sticks and moved across the courtyard. He sat down next to the hulk of a Galilean and in a very polite manner said, "Excuse me," then wagging a thumb toward the High Priest's house, "did you know him? The guy they arrested?"

Not a grumble or even a snore came back as an answer to his question from the brooding man.

"Excuse me," Moshie began again, "did you know him?" again pointing toward the house.

Again the silent response from the sulking man refused even to acknowledge Moshie's question.

"Certainly you were with him," Moshie began a third time, "I heard you talking earlier. You are a Galilean."

"Sir," began the curt reply, "you are mistaken."

"Look, I know you are one of the arrested Rabbi's friends, and I just wanted to know ..."

"I tell you ..."

"... wait, Omed the beggar was a friend of mine, and ..."

"Sir ..."

"... I just wanted to know what you believe ..."

"Get away from me."

"and," Moshie was desperately trying to finish, "who this Jesus is?"

"I don't know what you are talking about."

"And why you won't stick up for him?"

"Stick up for him? I don't even know him!"

As the cock crowed announcing the dawn, Moshie watched the man disappear around the corner of the yard and into the coldness of the red-skyed morning.

"Sorry!" Moshie yelled after the man. "It doesn't really matter anyway." Then quietly and with some reflection he said, "I just wanted to know more about Jesus. They'll most likely kill him, and with disciples like you, that will be the end of that."

"Wood, hey, wood for sale. Hey soldier, need some wood for that morning fire? Here let me re-kindle that for you. Have you been stationed in Jerusalem long? I'm from Antipatris, and I ..."

Order Of Service
Easter Sunday

Opening Words:
>L: Let us worship our Creator, the God of Love.
>
>**P: God continually preserves and sustains us.**
>
>L: We have been forgiven with a redeeming and eternal love.
>
>**P: Through the resurrection of Christ we have become witness to the full love of God.**

Hymn: "Come, Ye Faithful Raise The Strain" All

Prayer Of Confession: *(Unison)*
>We are hesitant to believe that good can emerge from the depths of tragedy and sin. Our hearts wander as we look for the proof of your love, O God. Life passes us by as we wait for you to respond to our wants. We make a good show of belief, but often our faith is hollow, a thin veneer. Find us in our restlessness, O God. Do not let us be the same as we fully grasp the significance of this resurrection day. Make us disciples. In the name of the risen one. Amen.

Assurance Of Pardon:
>Blessed are you when you seek the Lord. God has a way of finding us even when we are searching for something or someone else. Open yourself to what God has in store for you. The tomb opening for Christ opens to us the door to full and abundant life. Live as redeemed people.

Readings: Psalm 23; Acts 4:33-36; Luke 24:33-41

Hymn: "Thine Is The Glory" stanzas 1, 2

Meditation: Making Disciples

Hymn: "Thine Is The Glory" stanza 3

Service Of The Lord's Supper:

L: Let us affirm our faith.

P: We believe that the Lord Jesus Christ rose from the dead; that the suffering the world imposed upon him could not extinguish the love of God which burned in his heart. We believe that if we seek the Lord we shall be found by him. We thank God, our creator, sustainer, and redeemer, for all that has led us to the point and place of finding the love made full in Christ's life, teachings, death, burial and resurrection.

L: Lift up your hearts.

P: We lift them up to the Lord.

L: Let us give thanks to the Lord our God.

P: It is right and good that we give thanks and praise to God.

Prayers For Bread And Cup

The Distribution

Dismissal:

L: Keep us on the search, O God, as we leave this place. Renew us with thy Holy Spirit. Make us disciples.

P: Let us seek other disciples, that we may strengthen one another along the way.

L: Go in peace, knowing that you shall find your rest in the Lord.

P: May the Spirit lead us in joy.

Making Disciples
Easter Sunday

Acts 4:32-36

His hesitancy was not doubt. Not really. Unless, of course you consider the vague and haunting question of one's acceptability and worthiness as doubt. His hesitancy was not doubt, but whatever this feeling was, it made his heart skip and his step falter as he brought his gift for the upbuilding of the community to the feet of the apostles. He had no doubt that Jesus was the master teacher, was the Son of God, was the anointed one of Israel, was resurrected from the grave. He believed that Jesus was a new covenant that somehow made complete, somehow fulfilled, somehow made new and made sense of the law that Moses had given the people. His hesitancy was not doubt. It was that final struggle from within resolving on impulse, what had been (in a profound way) his plan.

Joseph had only intended to stay in Israel a short time when he arrived from Cyprus nine months ago. He had traveled to Israel for the Passover one occasion before, but this time he came to clear up some family business in the estate of his uncle and namesake, Joseph of Bethany. It was not a large inheritance, but it was property, and it felt very good and safe to be a land holder. His father had owned a business on Cyprus, not much really, but it had fallen into debt, had all assets liquidated and now the family simply worked in the shop and drew a small pension in addition to wages. But the pension stopped when his father died. Being an only child, and his mother having died while he was quite young, Joseph had no ties to Cyprus. He worked hard and had a bit more success than his father, but Joseph was discouraged by his lack of progress as well as his lack of profit. When the word came of his inheritance he quickly disposed of his household goods, sailed to Joppa, made the short trip inland to claim his inheritance, and become — well, he was not sure what he was to become.

While he told himself that he would celebrate the Passover in Jerusalem and then press on with his life, when he met his neighbors he decided that he might just stay a little longer. He quickly made friends with the neighbors, a man named Lazarus and two maiden sisters: Mary and Martha. Either of these two would make very fine wives, if the fates would be kind. One was wonderful in running the home, the other was exciting and vivacious and attractive and witty — which is not to say that the other was not, but that they were too wonderfully different women. Joseph was discouraged. How would he decide. Of course, he never considered that the two women would have any word on this matter.

It was in the home of Lazarus that Joseph met Jesus. A close friend of Lazarus was this Rabbi from Nazareth. He was both comfortable and uncomfortable with the way Jesus held with the law. The Cyprian part of him liked Jesus' less-nationalistic ways. Cyprian Jews were not Israelites. The Levite part of Joseph believed Jesus to be too brash in his interpretation of the law. Parables on a midrash are not Torah.

One night, amidst the stories that Jesus would tell (one of which humorously cast Lazarus as a poor beggar), he was asked about the law on inheritance and a problem that had arisen between two brothers. The answer was too clear, "A double share to the oldest, but who made me judge over you?" Jesus said, "Greed and generosity are controlled in the heart not the law. If the share is not enough for one it is not necessarily because the other has received too much." Jesus went on to tell a story about a farmer who expected a big crop but, after tearing down the barns, died. With no place to go the whole crop rotted in the field. "There is always," Jesus said, "a cost for attaining a larger share."

When Joseph heard these words he began to wonder if he had inherited the property in Bethany, or the property in Bethany had inherited him. He became discouraged. "This will never feel like home," Joseph thought to himself, "but I don't know where home can be."

He didn't know what to do. He could negotiate a contract for marriage with Lazarus for Martha. No, Mary. Well, if he could figure this one out he would become wealthy. Also, he was sure he would learn to love the one he picked. Well, maybe.

He could sell the land and go back to Cyprus. Return to work and someday buy another shop. There is great value in work. One knows who they are by the work they do. Well, maybe.

He could become an Essene and live at the Masada. No. On the day he thought about that John the Baptist was beheaded. No!

He could follow Jesus. But he didn't know where that would lead.

He came out of his door one morning and decided to go see Lazarus. He was not sure whether he would ask to negotiate a sale of his property to Lazarus or to negotiate a marriage contract. When he got to the door, however, Martha was crying. Lazarus had gotten deathly ill through the night.

"I'll go find Jesus," Joseph responded.

"We sent a servant through the night. Thank you." The door closed before he could ask if there was anything else he could do.

What a fool he had been. He wasn't part of their community. He was an outsider. He had attended a few dinners. He watched from a distance as the mourners came to the house. He sent a message of condolence. He shook their hands, stumbling for words that would not come in any language. He did enter the funeral procession. Watched as the big stone was rolled into place. Mary and Martha were inconsolable.

A couple of days later, having gathered his belongings, Joseph was on his way to see a lawyer about the sale of the property. He had just stepped out onto the street when Jesus passed him. The word spread fast that Jesus had come. Martha and Mary were out of the house for the first time in days. First one, then the other came to talk privately with Jesus.

Joseph could not bear it, and left town heading for the law office. He and his belongings would be on a ship in just a few days. The lawyer was nowhere to be found. "Did you hear," the clerk began, "that Jesus came ...?" "Yes, I heard. Mary knocked me down to get to him. He can have both of them. I will send for my money."

At a campsite half way to Joppa, travelers from Jerusalem told a tale of how a rich man from Bethany was brought from the grave by a Divine. In Joppa, Joseph discovered that the ship for Cyprus had left early that morning, the next ship to be in one week. As he sat in an inn waiting, Joseph heard tales of a parade of entrance into Jerusalem by a Rabbi and his followers.

Leaving his luggage in the care of the innkeeper, he went back to Bethany, sold the property to the lawyer and made it back to Joppa by Wednesday morning. That night at the inn he heard tales of a Rabbi taking a whip to the sellers in the temple.

Thursday, Joseph sold more of his belongings. None of his father's tools, but much of the baggage that had slowed him down the day he left Bethany.

The ship from Cyprus arrived Friday morning. In the afternoon a curious storm blew through. It frightened the ship's captain. The rumor started that a Rabbi named Jesus was arrested last night, betrayed by one of his own followers.

On Saturday afternoon while loading the belongings onto the ship for tomorrow morning's early tide departure, the news came that Jesus the Nazarene Rabbi had been executed by the Romans.

Joseph spent a miserable night. He tossed and turned and broke into sweat. Should he leave Israel? Should he go back to Cyprus? Should he open a new chapter of his life as if the last several months had not happened? At least his property did not own him anymore. Was that good or not? With Jesus dead would he have a chance to court Martha or Mary?

The wind began to move as the sky was split by streaking silver and gold rays of light. The sun had not yet appeared above the crest of the mountains, but the deep shadows of the night were fleeting. The steady creaking of the dock and the waves lapping on the side of the ship were interrupted by the clanging of the ship's bell, the hands heaving to, the canvas unfurling against the breeze, and the voice of one rising from a fitful sleep crying, "Wait, let me ashore, I cannot leave!"

Several hours of retrieving his belongings from the sea where the captain had thrown them overboard were followed by several days of chasing down the real story behind the events he had missed during the last week. In Bethany he found Lazarus alive and well. Mary and Martha had gone to Galilee with the followers of Jesus. As Joseph followed them to Galilee, they returned to Jerusalem. He finally caught up with the party outside Jerusalem, where he himself saw Jesus rise up into heaven, commanding them to preach and teach the good news, and baptize all in the assurance of his, and God's continued presence with them.

And then hearing in a clear Cyprian language the preaching of Peter that Jesus was the Messiah, Joseph became one of 3,000 who dedicated their lives to the fact of Jesus' Messiahship. When he was baptized at the hand of Peter, he knew what was to become of him. He didn't know how, he didn't know what would happen, where he would go, or if he would marry, he only knew that he could not allow the inheritance of the property in Bethany to own him, for he belonged to Jesus Christ. He took the bag of silver and gold coins and gave it to Peter saying, "I trust you to do with this as seems fit for the community of the faithful. I do not know what I will do with my life, but it begins here and now, and I give my all to you."

Peter dropped the money bag on the floor and took Joseph by the hand.

"Joseph, you are a man of many moods," Peter said. "We have seen you wondering, sad, excited, depressed. You know better than most how hard it is to come to this decision;

the many trials we go through. So I want you to help us by helping others when they get depressed. Since I see in you the possibility of helping others, I am going to call you my son of encouragement. Barnabas.

www.ingramcontent.com/pod-product-compliance
Lightning Source LLC
Chambersburg PA
CBHW060853050426
42453CB00008B/964